W9-AZQ-720

FOREVER MY LOVE

FOREVER MY LOVE

NEIL CLARK WARREN, PH.D.

TYNDALE HOUSE PUBLISHERS, INC.
WHEATON, ILLINOIS

Visit Tyndale's exciting Web site at www.tyndale.com

Cover designed by Paetzold Design

Interior designed by Jackie Noe

Quotations by Neil Clark Warren, Ph.D., are taken from *The Triumphant Marriage: 100 Extremely Successful Couples Reveal Their Secrets,* copyright © 1995 by Neil Clark Warren (Colorado Springs: Focus on the Family). Used by permission of Focus on the Family.

Scripture quotations marked KJV are taken from the *Holy Bible,* King James Version.

Scripture quotations marked "NKJV" are taken from the New King James Version. Copyright © 1979, 1980, 1982 by Thomas Nelson, Inc. Used by permission. All rights reserved.

Scripture quotations marked NASB are taken from the *New American Standard Bible,* © 1960, 1962, 1963, 1968, 1971, 1972, 1973, 1975, 1977 by The Lockman Foundation. Used by permission.

Scripture quotations marked NIV are taken from the *Holy Bible,* New International Version®. NIV®. Copyright © 1973, 1978, 1984 by International Bible Society. Used by permission of Zondervan Publishing House. All rights reserved.

ISBN 0-8423-1782-1

Printed in the United States of America

04   03   02   01   00   99   98
7   6   5   4   3   2   1

CONTENTS

INTRODUCTION
The Triumphant Marriage

There are 107 million married persons in the United States, and most of them want a better marriage. They want their marriage to be deeper and stronger, more fulfilling and dependable. They want to feel better bonded with their mate, more consistently "in sync"; they want to know that their marriage is on its way to being healthier and more exciting.

This book is designed to help people make their marriages magnificent. Why? Because marriage is the greatest institution ever invented! It can be good, or it can be great, but it should never be ordinary. Your marriage can be moved closer and closer to the highest level of satisfaction—to a level I refer to as *triumphant*. If your marriage is triumphant, it will be a winner. It will overcome every last obstacle that stands in the way of its total success.

This book will show you how to make your marriage the best it can be—and encourage you to celebrate each step of the way!

NEIL CLARK WARREN, PH.D.

PART ONE

The Heart of
INTIMACY

The fundamental purpose of marriage is to provide a context in which a deeper, purer, richer form of love can be enjoyed—and love is all about intimacy, passion, and commitment.

Part of the reason for this revolves around how we're built. There is a profound sense in most of us that we can know a deeper level of love and a greater sense of completeness when we find that person of the opposite sex with whom we can enjoy a life-changing experience. When a man finds his woman and a woman finds her man, all they need for a magnificent union are the insight and skill involved in developing intimacy, passion, and commitment.

Any union in which these "secrets of love" provide the yarn out of which the marriage fabric is woven promises a significantly better reward for time and energy investments than any other human enterprise.

[Love] bears all things, believes all things,

hopes all things, endures all things.

Love never fails. . . . Now abide

faith, hope, love, these three;

but the greatest of these is love.

1 CORINTHIANS 13:7-8, 13, NASB

THE CENTRAL ROLE OF LOVE

*E*very marriage expert knows that hard work and determination aren't the only ingredients that lead to a great marriage. Some couples work incredibly hard on their marriages, but they are left hungering for something significantly better.

The critical question about every marriage is a question about *love!* Whether a marriage becomes great or not depends entirely on whether two people learn to love each other well—whether they learn love's secrets and develop the necessary skills to implement them. This kind of love can energize a marriage and fill it with vitality and health. It can create a relationship that will make the marital life supremely worth living—even when problems arise. The payoff for those who learn how to really love is a level of human experience beyond our fondest dreams.

Therefore shall a man leave

his father and his mother,

and shall cleave unto his wife:

and they shall be one flesh.

Genesis 2:24, kjv

*T*hose who enter marriage should expect a relational situation requiring all kinds of change and growth. The very thrill of marriage involves meeting the challenges and improving your relationship.

The principle challenge of marriage is the weaving together of two complex individual identities and the forming of a corporate identity. The building of a corporate identity, or oneness, is particularly attractive because it offers the potential to meet basic, individual needs in a far more deeply satisfying way than they have ever been met before. But the formation of the corporate identity requires significant flexibility and elasticity on the part of both individuals. Continual negotiation and compromise are essential.

The strongest message married people need to hear is that, the more complex their individual identities, the greater the challenges are likely to be. But at the same time, the more differentiated they are as persons, the greater their potential for weaving together a corporate identity that will be rich with variation, breadth, and satisfaction.

The Lord is my rock and my fortress

and my deliverer, my God, my rock,

in whom I take refuge;

my shield and the horn of my salvation,

my stronghold.

PSALM 18:2, NASB

THE IMPORTANCE OF WILLPOWER

I've never seen happier, more deeply satisfied people than men and women who have made their marriages work. But neither have I met many people in highly successful marriages who got there without an enormous expenditure of energy and courage and determination.

Virtually every successful marriage requires all kinds of willpower. The foundation of willpower is a set of strong marital promises that serve as the steel structure of every great marriage.

Sometimes issues arise, and the partners don't have the necessary skills to manage them. They essentially have two choices: give up and run away, or get about the task of developing the required skills.

Partners with willpower wouldn't think of giving up. They know that marriage doesn't just happen! It takes a solid set of decisions, a huge amount of skill, and enormous willpower. They build their marriages just as you build a mammoth bridge or a skyscraper. The backbreaking work doesn't matter; their willpower gives them this kind of toughness.

Give ear and come to me; hear me,

that your soul may live.

I will make an everlasting covenant with you,

my faithful love promised to David.

Isaiah 55:3, niv

THE CORNERSTONE OF COMMITMENT

*O*ne of the chief determinants of your marital strength is the degree to which your promises to your spouse are current—that is, the degree to which you passionately affirm your marital vows *today*.

Commitment is more than "sticking it out." It requires a far more active approach in marriage—and certainly during a time of marital challenge. It's active rather than passive.

The radical part of the commitment vow is that you promise to *love* the other person through every kind of circumstance for as long as you both live. Moreover, you promise to *honor* and *cherish* your mate. Not only that, but you also promise to perform every duty that a husband or wife owes to their spouse as long as you both live. So there are four huge promises that you make to your spouse—all of which are highly active, all of which involve only *your* action, all of which you make unilaterally and unequivocally for as long as you live—no matter what!

He will call upon me, and I will answer him;

I will be with him in trouble,

I will deliver him and honor him.

PSALM 91:15, NIV

*I*f you analyze the traditional marriage vows, you will discover six separate parts:

1. I will love you as long as we both live.

2. I will cherish you as long as we both live.

3. I will honor you as long as we both live.

4. I will be for you everything that a husband or wife owes to their spouse.

5. I will never give my love to, or get romantically involved with, another person.

6. I will do all five of these things under every kind of condition for as long as we live.

The marriage vow says that if my wife and I don't agree about something, I promise to take her position seriously and to honor her, even in the midst of her disagreement. If I don't get what I think I need from her, I promise not to withhold anything I owe her, and I promise to remain loyal to her. My promises do not mean that I will ignore our differences or fail to stand up for my own thoughts, feelings, and rights, but they do mean that I will never stop loving her, honoring her, and cherishing her, no matter what.

And Adam said,

This is now bone of my bones,

and flesh of my flesh:

she shall be called Woman,

because she was taken out of Man.

GENESIS 2:23, KJV

INCREASING YOUR INTIMACY

*M*y wife and I have some close friends who are deeply intimate with each other. We admire their level of intimacy every time we are with them. The content of their interactions isn't always positive; after all, intimacy is about the sharing of the innermost thoughts and feelings, and those almost always contain both positive and negative aspects. The couple simply tells each other whatever they think and feel at any given moment.

That's the freedom two persons have when they deeply trust each other. It is the freedom to "be themselves" in the relationship, and this ability is at the heart of intimacy.

This kind of sharing allows two lovers to interweave themselves with each other, to fashion a whole new corporate being, which the Bible refers to as "one flesh." This new partnership can satisfy so many fundamental needs for togetherness—and the wonder of togetherness is that the actualization of two individual selves can be accomplished in the most basic and profound ways. All of this rich and healthy relating happens only within an atmosphere of trust.

Teach me your way, O Lord,

and I will walk in your truth.

TELLING THE TRUTH

*T*ell the truth! It all starts here. A marriage has so much to gain if both partners can rest assured that the truth, the whole truth, and nothing but the truth is the intended goal of every message they give each other.

There are three levels on which truth-telling is crucial. The first is the *verbal* level. There must be no lies!

Second, truth is crucial on the *behavioral* level. Both marital partners need to become known as people who do what they promise they'll do.

Third, it's important to be truthful on the *being* level. Each partner needs to be himself, or be herself, in order to contribute to the relationship. Want a healthy marriage? Then tell the truth every chance you get. Talk the truth, behave the truth, and be the truth. If you do this, you will become known as a person of integrity. When your lover relates to you, he or she will know exactly who you are. There will be no need for guessing games. You and your partner can be genuine and authentic, completely free to be your true selves at the deepest and most profound levels.

Let love and faithfulness never leave you;

bind them around your neck,

write them on the tablet of your heart.

Then you will win favor and a good name

in the sight of God and man.

PROVERBS 3:3-4, NIV

MAXIMIZING TRUST

*Y*ou want to build a triumphant marriage? Maximize the trust factor in your relationship.

Marriages in which two people trust each other at the deepest levels have at least five priceless assets. First, they have emotional insurance that provides support and stability through all the hard times of life. Second, they don't have to worry about failure; if they fail, their companion will still be unconditionally faithful. Third, they don't have to spend any of their time or energy being suspicious; there is total freedom in total trust. Fourth, they are assured that every investment they make in this partnership will pay dividends— and that it will last. Finally, they can have genuine peace of mind: the prize for those who are deeply committed to each other for a lifetime.

So build a totally trustworthy partnership, and then prepare to move with rocketlike speed to a heart of intimacy in your marriage.

For God hath not given us the spirit of fear;

but of power, and of love,

and of a sound mind.

2 TIMOTHY 1:7, KJV

*B*elieve me, I know marriage can provide profound happiness. But there's an unfortunate expectation that permeates our society—that a good marriage will, under virtually all circumstances, make the two individuals involved happy.

However, partners don't find happiness just by *being married.* They must first be happy in who they are individually. All emotional health starts with a person's self-concept. If your positive sense of self allows you the freedom to deal with life fully—that is, to perceive accurately all the facets of your internal and external life—you are well on your way to health. If you also know how to stand in the middle of all these facets and make good, solid decisions that will benefit both your life and your loved one's life, then you are likely to end up very healthy—and the intimacy level of your marriage will be boosted as well.

It all starts with a great self-conception.

How beautiful you are

and how pleasing,

O love, with your delights!

SONG OF SONGS 7:6, NIV

*W*hen a marriage involves two people who experience strong chemistry, the relationship has fuel in its tank.

Having passion and chemistry is vital if you want a triumphant marriage. Good, solid, steady, durable chemistry between two marriage partners is an incredibly valuable asset.

Chemistry makes everything about the marriage work better. When it's present, people get along better, they work together more effectively, and they resolve conflicts with less pain. They not only want to be around one another, they also want to hold hands, sit together in one slightly oversized chair, hug one another, and say all kinds of "sweet nothings" to each other.

But here's a surprise: Chemistry between two people is responsive to mental and emotional processes over which we have tremendous control. In other words, if you don't feel the flutter in your heart for your spouse that you once did—if the magic is gone from your relationship—don't panic. You can change that—you can make chemistry happen!

That their hearts may be encouraged, having been knit together in love, and attaining to all the wealth that comes from the full assurance of understanding, resulting in a true knowledge of God's mystery, that is, Christ Himself.

Colossians 2:2, nasb

When a person experiences one of his or her fundamental needs being met by another person, he or she suddenly begins to feel more intimate with the "need meeter." Take self-esteem, for instance. We all have a strong need to feel good about ourselves. When we are around someone who makes us feel more positively about ourselves, our chemistry in relation to this person will grow. It doesn't matter much what the need is that gets satisfied; the crucial thing is that a particular individual helps us get this need met. When this happens, the magic begins.

I often encourage married people to figure out exactly what needs their mates have. It's even best to rank them from what you perceive to be most important to the least important.

The crucial point is simply this: One way to increase your heart of intimacy is to get organized in your thinking about your spouse's needs and then to set about meeting them as fully as you know how.

I am my beloved's,

and his desire is toward me.

Song of Solomon 7:10, KJV

BUILDING A GREAT SEX LIFE

The best sexual relationship is one that proceeds out of a couple's deep and intimate "soul bonding." Show me a couple for whom feelings and thoughts are shared from the innermost levels, and I'll show you a couple ready to have a triumphant sexual relationship. If their sexual relationship is not triumphant, they probably only need some careful instruction and coaching.

It is spiritual bonding that characterizes the finest marital relationships. Spiritual bonding comes from hard work that is carried out in an atmosphere of deep trust. When spiritual bonding is established, sex is a lot more than the merging of body parts. What really happens is that the souls of two people get woven together. This is even more important than orgasm, but orgasm is likely to happen when the spiritual bond develops. This is when euphoria is experienced!

PART TWO

The Harmonizing of
DREAMS

Dreaming and envisioning are the essence of romance! Show me a couple who dreams about their future together—or tells someone else about their dreams—and I will show you a couple who is deeply in love. People who help each other access and focus their individual and corporate dreams are vital to one another. There is nothing in the world so attractive as someone who will dream with us, merge their dreams with our own, clarify the path toward the actualization of the dream, and lock their arms with ours while walking the path.

The harmonizing of dreams is an essential part of the process of capturing a marital vision. The best marriages I know involve two people who have a well-formed vision of the life they are pursuing together. They thoroughly enjoy dreaming together—and planning a way to make their dreams come true.

✳

Be strong and courageous!

Do not tremble or be dismayed,

for the Lord your God

is with you wherever you go.

Joshua 1:9, NASB

WHY DREAM?

*D*reams and visions stimulate the brain and mobilize the action centers. Whatever it is that you dream about with regularity, you will begin to hope for. Hope stimulates planning. Planning produces behavior designed to move you forward. This brings progress. It all begins with a dream!

When two people dream and envision together, they merge the resources of their deepest, most positive centers. They each have tremendous personal power when they access the core emotions and longings in their individual centers. When they pool this power and focus it for the benefit of all three of them—each of them individually and the two of them as a couple—they become significantly stronger than they could be as two separate individuals.

It is this corporate strength that contributes to the greatness and the excitement of marriage. When this strength is mobilized, the partners are able to overcome momentary adversity, withstand temporary stalemates, push temptations aside, and prove victorious over every kind of difficulty.

Commit to the Lord whatever you do,

and your plans will succeed.

PROVERBS 16:3, NIV

PLANNING YOUR COURSE

*E*very couple needs to take conscious responsibility for choosing the course their marriage will follow. Goodness knows that their marriage will follow some course—even if it's around in circles. And the best course is likely to be the one they choose together at every point along the way.

It's important to envision your lives together five, ten, or fifteen years ahead. Even the best of marital visions grows stale and out of date. A reworking of the vision is a continual necessity. Sometimes, complete remodeling rather than merely redecoration is required.

The point is that both partners need to be strongly committed to their marital dream and "on board" together. When you begin to sense a deeply shared commitment to the dream, you start believing in the dream's power to do great things for the marriage.

And we know that all things work together for good to those who love God, to those who are the called according to His purpose.

ROMANS 8:28, NKJV

*S*ome of the partners in the one hundred highly successful marriages I've studied said that they "simply try to live their lives one day at a time." The "one day at a time" is a slogan that governs their thinking, but the health of their marriages indicates that all kinds of other "agreements" about the future have been worked out with their spouses. They actually have a very well-worked-out vision for how they conduct their lives.

For instance, they get up every morning and do all kinds of things for each other. She gets coffee for both of them, and he gets the newspaper. She takes some meat out of the freezer for dinner, and he calls the travel agent about their trip next month. They are living their life one day at a time, but their coordination in the midst of complexity is often the result of a quiet, unassuming vision of their life together—a purposeful vision that guides them into the future, even if that future is only the next few hours.

Yes, I have loved you with an everlasting love;

therefore with lovingkindness I have drawn you.

Jeremiah 31:3, NKJV

*C*ouples who truly love each other and want a healthy marriage ask themselves this question, Is the dream equally inclusive of me, my spouse, and our life together?

At the center of dreaming and planning should be a constantly recurring theme: "I want the future to be good for you. If it is not good for you, it cannot be good for us. Whatever is healthy and good for you, we will find a way to make it work in our life together."

Do you hear that theme? "I want it to be good for *you!*" Being cared for this way, if it is unselfish and mutual, is at the core of romance.

God shall supply all your needs

according to His riches in glory

in Christ Jesus.

PHILIPPIANS 4:19, NASB

IDENTIFYING YOUR NEEDS

*D*reams are partially masked strategies designed to meet basic needs. Values are considerations that help us determine the long-term effect of pursuing a given strategy for the satisfaction of one of our needs.

One value that has been proven over and over concerns the superficial internal effects of accumulating material things. Specifically, the need to feel important usually doesn't get met when the dream of becoming wealthy comes true.

Identifying which dreams you want to dream together is a big part of the joy and excitement that comes from the enterprise. The relationship takes on real substance in the process of both people discovering their basic needs, developing the dreams that are designed to provide the satisfaction for those needs, and then checking out the congruence of those dreams with their individual value systems.

Commit your way to the Lord;

trust in him.

PSALM 37:5, NIV

COMMITTING YOURSELF—PERSONALLY

*O*bviously, a vision for the future of your marriage will be significantly stronger if both spouses are involved in formulating and actualizing it. But scores of marriages have taken on new strength on the basis of just one person's active dreaming and praying for the marriage.

When that one person becomes crystal clear about a great and worthy vision for his or her life and marriage, and when that person sets his or her mind in the direction of the chosen destination, all kinds of good things can happen.

What courage it takes to give everything you have in an effort to make your marriage better—even when your spouse hangs back. But if you are the one longing for a far better marriage, don't give up! Work to make *your* vision a reality. You may be surprised at the dramatic results.

I will bless thee,

and make thy name great;

and thou shalt be a blessing.

Genesis 12:2, KJV

BROADENING THE DREAM

*I*s your dream broad enough? By this I mean does it cover enough of the totality of life?

There's nothing wrong with having kids, buying a nice house, achieving career success, and traveling to far-off places. But there may be something narrow and superficial about the experience of reaching these goals.

Have you given thought to the development of the spiritual sides of your future? Does your journey-together dream give plenty of weight to your skill for sharing more and more generously with each other from the deepest parts of your inner lives?

Also, is there a place for service to less fortunate people and to your community? To produce a brilliant marriage, the dream must be broad enough to include others and deep enough to reach the spiritual realm.

The Lord is good to those

whose hope is in him,

to the one who seeks him.

LAMENTATIONS 3:25, NIV

ENRICHING YOUR MARITAL DREAMS

*I*t is easy in a demanding world for two people who are married to become distant and lost. Formulating a vision for your future together is an exercise that every couple needs to engage in—and preferably every year.

So set some time aside and do the following:

1. Picture yourselves in the future. What will your life be like in ten years—and what challenges will you likely face? Kids in college? Aging parents?

2. Spend time together thinking about where each of you would like to be in the next ten years and where you would like your marriage to be.

3. Next, prepare a chart showing that ten-year period, broken down into six-month segments. Enter your vision as you hope it'll unfold over time. Ten years can become such a short period when you introduce your goals.

4. Then list any obstacles you expect to encounter, and devise a way to deal with each of the challenges.

5. Finally, each of you write a page about how you will feel—ten years from now—if your plan is realized. And get ready for some exciting, visionary reading full of hopes and dreams!

I do not regard myself as having laid hold of it yet; but one thing I do: forgetting what lies behind and reaching forward to what lies ahead, I press on toward the goal for the prize of the upward call of God in Christ Jesus.

PHILIPPIANS 3:13-14, NASB

GOING FOR THE GOAL

A brilliant marriage can be built by any two people who are willing to learn and practice until they're very good at the relationship.

If you're motivated to work on your marriage, your marriage can grow dramatically. So as you dream together and grow closer together, your marriage can become 10 percent better this next year and every year thereafter. And the results could be even greater than that!

This country could certainly use a few hundred thousand solid, healthy, fulfilling marriages; yours could be one of them. So dream with your spouse about setting your sights on a brilliant marriage. Then go after the prize with every ounce of determination and courage you have. And don't stop until your marriage is well on its way to greatness!

Know thou the God of thy father,

and serve him with a perfect heart

and with a willing mind:

for the Lord searcheth all hearts,

and understandeth all the

imaginations of the thoughts.

1 CHRONICLES 28:9, KJV

*A*ll of us have access to an incredible computer . . . and it's located right between our ears. I have watched people put this computer to a test, and the results have been startling. Yet I suspect that most of us utilize far too little of our brain's capacity when it comes to envisioning our own future, the future of the person we love more than all others, and our corporate future with this person.

The brain can not only conceive big dreams but also help us plan to achieve them. Develop a big plan for your life together, and then get about the thoroughly enjoyable task of setting your brain free to plan and achieve the well-designed marital estate you have envisioned.

Magnificent marriages involve two people who dream magnificently. The partners encourage each other to dig deeper and dream bigger, and in the process they get in touch with a level of being and doing that otherwise would be far beyond them.

Write down the revelation

and make it plain on tablets.

HABAKKUK 2:2, NIV

WRITING DOWN YOUR VISION

Wherever you are in your marriage currently, I am convinced that any investment you make in building a great dream for you and your partner will pay generous dividends. I encourage you to think long and hard about the kind of life that will provide for each of you individually—and for the two of you together—the level of satisfaction you seek. I have two friends who carry the following vision in their wallets at all times:

"We hereby commit ourselves to the following: (1) to love each other under every circumstance for as long as we live; (2) to search after meaning and satisfaction together wherever it may be found; (3) to support and encourage each other at every turn of life; (4) to love our kids generously and personally, and to raise them wisely; (5) to be involved in serving others, especially the underprivileged; (6) to respond actively and enthusiastically to the love and guidance of God."

What's your marital vision?

PART THREE

Putting Thoughts and Feelings into
WORDS

Think for a minute about the complexity of marriage. Two unique individuals form a contract with each other. Each of them has an elaborate inner world of thoughts and feelings, goals and dreams, values and opinions, wounds and sensitivities—not to mention a few million needs.

When they get together and become "one flesh," it's not without a lot of banging and clanging, conflicting and crying, talking and sharing, merging and blending. Not without a lot of simple, straightforward communication!

Working it out so that "my two million" and "your two million" get along requires an enormous amount of masterful negotiation and adaption. But the goal—one flesh, one spirit, one identity, one mission—is well worth the work it takes to develop good communication.

It's my conviction that a marriage is about as healthy as the level of communication that transpires within it.

Be kind and compassionate to one another, forgiving

each other, just as in Christ God forgave you.

EPHESIANS 4:32, NIV

GETTING DOWN THE BASICS

*M*arital communication is simple if you and your spouse know how to do it, if you can do it in the sunshine of a spring day when the two of you agree on everything, if you do it when you're focused on each other, and if you do it when you're rested and peaceful. But communication isn't always so simple—life can be stressful.

However, in essence, communication is simply talking and listening. But the matter becomes decidedly more challenging when the relative amount that you talk and I talk gets raised. What about the pace of our discussion? How long do you get to talk before I do? Who gets to talk the loudest? And when you listen, could you look me in the eye? Why is it that when I talk you seem like a tiger poised to jump in every time I leave a nanosecond between words?

The good news is that virtually any couple can learn to master communication—and thereby improve their marriage. It just takes strong motivation and endless practice. And we need to do it in such a way that both people feel heard, understood, affirmed, and valued.

I say to every man among you not to think more highly

of himself than he ought to think;

but to think so as to have sound judgment.

ROMANS 12:3, NASB

COMMUNICATION QUALITIES OF HEALTHY PEOPLE

*S*even qualities stand out:

1. They aren't desperate to impress others. Their inner conviction that they are "worthy of enormous respect" is so deeply established that even what you think or say about them doesn't shake what they know to be true.

2. They don't need to be perfect. They realize how often they, and others, fall short.

3. They are not hesitant—or defensive—about using professional resources. And they don't mind telling you about the help they received.

4. They don't judge your worth on external factors. They relate to you as a person created by God and worthy of respect.

5. They overcome major problems with even greater solutions, turning tragedy into triumph.

6. They emphasize the spiritual dimension. Thus, they experience inner peace, even in the face of trials.

7. They focus on others instead of themselves. They are free from the need to promote themselves.

Two healthy people of such qualities are in line for the greatest marriage they can imagine!

The Lord is my shepherd, I shall not be in want.

He makes me lie down in green pastures,

he leads me beside quiet waters, he restores my soul.

He guides me in paths of righteousness

for his name's sake.

PSALM 23:1–3, NIV

*G*reat communication seldom happens in the middle of complexity. A ringing phone can kill the development of a theme. Kids running in and out of the room with their needs and their troubles and their ordinary play can make communication disjointed and superficial. Moreover, great communication seldom takes place when stress is heavy, when neediness is running high, or when the situation is satiated with demands for quick decisions and emergency measures.

What you and your spouse need is plenty of plain old wonderful time. Quiet, uninterrupted, unhurried, stress-free time. Maybe you need to take a long walk together or meet at the park for a picnic lunch together or take a trip together.

The bottom line is simply this: The value of communication and the intimacy gained from it is greatly affected by the context in which it takes place. If that context is characterized by time away from the heavy demands of your routine lives, allowing you to relax and tap into the peaceful, thoughtful parts of yourselves, then your communication—indeed, your entire marriage—is sure to benefit dramatically.

There is no fear in love;

but perfect love casteth out fear.

1 JOHN 4:18, KJV

MAKING THE MOST OF CONFLICT

To have a great marriage, there must be two authentic partners. Authenticity involves the full and free expression of each person's true self, with all of its uniqueness. When both people are fully authentic, their complete agreement on everything is highly unlikely. Some conflict is inevitable.

The wonderful thing you do for your marriage is to share that part of you that is different from your mate. This is the kind of healthy conflict that gives you the opportunity to expand your marriage. Together you can build a marriage strategy that's designed to expand the boundaries of your life together and to increase the interest range of your relationship.

So if you want to sit still in your marriage, rule out all conflict. Well-managed conflict is like a stairway that can lead you to higher and higher levels of marital greatness. So recognize marriage as a "we" business, process data as quickly as possible, stick to the subject, don't intimidate each other, don't name-call, turn up your listening sensitivity, practice give-and-take, and celebrate every victory—together.

I will help you speak

and will teach you what to say.

EXODUS 4:12, NIV

PUTTING THOUGHTS AND FEELINGS INTO WORDS

*S*ome people don't talk much, but they feel a lot! They just don't know how to put all their thoughts and feelings, needs and yearnings into words, phrases, and sentences. It requires a lot of skill, and most skills require a lot of practice.

Learning to access your inner meanings is a big part of communication. But learning how to put those meanings into words is equally important. Children who learn this skill from their parents are blessed indeed. If you weren't taught by parents, you have to learn some way—with the help of a counselor, trusted friend, or your mate.

It may be that when you first attempt to put your feelings into words you will feel awkward and clumsy. But people who talk together, who work to develop their communication skills, speed their growth in every other area of their marriage as well.

Therefore encourage one another,

and build up one another.

1 THESSALONIANS 5:11, NASB

FIVE WAYS TO IMPROVE YOUR COMMUNICATION—IMMEDIATELY!

*I*f you want to strengthen your communication, try these suggestions:

1. Ask your spouse how her day is going, and really focus on the answer. Plan to stay with the subject for five minutes or so. Ask two or three follow-up questions. Show real interest.

2. Turn off the television, put life on "pause," and take time to refresh your relationship after a tiring day. Any couple who takes even a half hour every day to check in, discuss anything and everything, is going to see dramatic improvement in their communication.

3. Send a note or gift for no particular reason—with a heartfelt message.

4. Find a way to get the communication flowing. Engage in an activity that takes some time. Use that time to explore in depth a subject that ordinarily doesn't get addressed.

5. If there's a crisis for either one of you, make sure you move right in on it. No business deal, television program, or church event is as important as a crisis affecting your spouse.

Listen to advice and accept instruction,

and in the end you will be wise.

PROVERBS 19:20, NIV

BECOMING A GREAT LISTENER

*L*istening seems so easy, but in my experience, very few people know how to listen well. Show me a good listener, and I'll show you someone who makes everybody they know better talkers.

I believe that virtually every marriage in North America would be several times better if the two people simply improved their listening skills. I venture to say that more wonderful moments are experienced in marriage because two people learn how to really listen to one another than because of any other one thing. Something magical happens inside of most people when they are listened to. Marital partners can work their way through complex marital entanglements—just because they are listening to each other. There is phenomenal power that gets activated because of listening.

When we listen, it means that we are taking each other seriously—that we are on level playing ground and that we consider the other person as important.

I pray that the fellowship of your faith
may become effective through the
knowledge of every good thing
which is in you for Christ's sake.

Philemon 1:6, NASB

THE POWER OF EMPATHY

*E*mpathy gives the dialogue of marriage a big lift. It's about trying to see and experience the world the way the other person does. In that moment, you put yourself in your spouse's position. You make every effort to understand from his or her viewpoint everything that is said.

Empathy doesn't come cheap. It requires a decision that you're going to do it—for as long as the encounter lasts. That means tuning out on yourself. Even then, it's no easy thing to understand another's messages just the way that person means them. You will need to watch for visual clues and listen for auditory nuances. Then, in order to find out if you really understand or not, you will need to say what you have heard, to the best of your ability.

Empathy takes a lot of energy, it demands a lot of hard work, and there's some real risk in it. There's nothing easy about trying to understand the complex, inner world of another human being. But it is at the heart of great communication.

Let them do good,

that they be rich in good works,

ready to give, willing to share,

storing up for themselves

a good foundation for the time to come,

that they may lay hold on eternal life.

1 Timothy 6:18–19, NKJV

JUMP-STARTING YOUR COMMUNICATION

*T*here's a simple exercise that will greatly enhance any couple's communication. You and your spouse should pick two half-hour time slots per week to get together just to talk. It's best if these times can be the same each week. Also, get away from the telephone and other potential interruptions. Maybe you can take a walk or a drive.

I recommend that you work on the same exercise for several weeks or months. Spend exactly one half hour talking and listening. If it seems reasonable to you, take turns starting the sessions. One of you should talk about something that matters to you. Don't talk too long, but address your topic thoroughly. Your partner doesn't get to say anything in response until he has repeated in his own words what you said, and you can say "that's correct." Then it's his turn to respond. This process is continued for the entire half hour.

This exercise will improve your communication skills substantially. And as you make progress, hope and momentum will build in you.

Many waters cannot quench love,

neither can the floods drown it.

SONG OF SOLOMON 8:7, KJV

CREATIVE WAYS TO SAY YOUR VOWS—AGAIN

I will love you when times are good or bad. I will cherish you even if I am upset with you. I will honor you at all times." Every couple can profit from saying these simple words to each other every day. The more each person can find new and creative ways to swear to this commitment, the better. For instance, some part of it can be put into a lunch sack, engraved inside a bracelet, scribbled on a refrigerator note in the morning, contained in a love letter, or written in the sky above a football game.

The idea is to recite this vow over and over so that when the rocky times come, as they inevitably will, and when the flat places appear, as they inevitably will, the commitment to love, honor, and cherish will trigger new ideas in the brain about how to hold the marriage together.

Periodic rewrites of the commitment statement and verbalizing it will make it even stronger. And new ways of living out the commitment—beyond verbalizing it—will wind its meaning around the bedrock of your soul.

Behold, you are fair, my love!

Behold, you are fair!

SONG OF SOLOMON 4:1, NKJV

SHARING YOUR EMOTIONS

I believe that the wonder of marriage involves the sharing of emotions at the deepest levels. This is what first-class communication makes possible. You and the person you love more than anyone in the world can become known to each other so far below the surface that you will never have experienced such closeness before.

Communication is crucial to the vitality in any relationship. Here's what I know for sure: Any couple who will work hard to talk to each other from the heart and listen to each other with a curiosity born of genuine love will move at a faster and faster pace toward a triumphant marriage. It boils down to the fact that a loving relationship almost always involves regular sharing. There is nothing in the world that binds two lovers together more effectively than this. It takes willpower to keep it going day after day, but when it becomes habitual, it is the source of virtually everything wonderful in a marriage.

PART FOUR

The Blessing of

CHILDREN

Over ninety of one hundred couples surveyed stressed the vital contribution to their marriages that their children had made.

Everybody knows that children require backbreaking work from the time they push their little heads out of the birth canal and say hello to this big world. So what in the world makes them so important to a great marriage?

Because of the way biology works, there is no other means by which two lovers can merge so profoundly as they do in their children. If merging and blending are at the heart of the love experience, then children make love happen between two people at levels that are otherwise impossible. Every cell of this child is made up of us. Every propensity is the result of our combined essence. There is something about knowing all this that sends romantic shivers down our spines.

Children represent, both biologically and emotionally, the fusion of our beings. It is this fusion that contributes so significantly to the sacredness of marriage.

Therefore know that the Lord your God, He is God,

the faithful God who keeps covenant and mercy

for a thousand generations

with those who love Him

and keep His commandments.

DEUTERONOMY 7:9, NKJV

CHILDREN—A UNIQUE BLEND

After years of listening to people talk about their children, I've become convinced married couples are passionate about the blending of both spouses' physical, emotional, and intellectual qualities. It's the magical combination of "half my genes and half yours." There's something mind-boggling about the idea that we can somehow merge our uniqueness—our very beings—in a little person who will live with us and be around us for the rest of our lives. And this little being will be an incredible blend of you and me. We can have a little us.

When you encounter the mystery of human life—the essence of "one flesh" in our children—from an up-close vantage point, you cannot fail to sense the powerful presence of God. Children are clear evidence that God has taken the essence of you and me and made us "one flesh."

As parents participate together in the formation of beautiful young lives, they experience a deep sense of oneness with each other.

And they shall be My people,

and I will be their God;

and I will give them one heart and one way,

that they may fear Me always,

for their own good, and for the good

of their children after them.

JEREMIAH 32:38–39, NASB

BECOMING EQUAL PARTNERS

I encourage parents to recognize what a vital part child rearing can play in their lives together. When they take it on as partners, when they see what a sacred privilege it is, when they come to recognize that rearing great kids is a goal worth pursuing, they are headed toward something wonderful. Children contribute greatly to a triumphant marriage if a man and woman are equal partners in the task, if they both deeply love their offspring, and if they recognize that sometimes the energy required to meet the demands will take everything they've got.

This is the big picture that a husband and a wife need to be clear about. If they are, they will be able to rise to the challenge—and thoroughly enjoy the process. And when they stand back to marvel at their kids, they will secretly be saying to each other: "Oh, my, hasn't this been wonderful? How very much I love you when I look at these children of ours. This partnership of ours is such a strong and healthy one."

I said, "I will go up to the palm tree,

I will take hold of its branches."

Let now your breasts be like clusters of the vine

the fragrance of your breath like apples,

and the roof of your mouth like the best wine.

Song of Solomon 7:8-9, nkjv

FINDING TIME FOR ROMANCE

*S*how me a man and a woman who have children, and I will show you a man and a woman who need more than ever to nurture their relationship and make sure it thrives and grows.

There is something about romance that is intensely personal. It all gets started when two people look at each other and feel something powerful inside. Two lovers never outgrow their need to look at one another, share with each other from the most central part of themselves, and be assured that the other person cherishes them and respects them.

Romance requires personal time. There is never a time when two people can keep their love growing and prospering without plenty of energy spent relating to each other individually and intimately.

That is why I encourage people who have children—especially small children or adolescents—to schedule time for their romance, to make time for it at least once a week. This time investment will pay incredible dividends.

The mercy of the Lord

is from everlasting to everlasting

on those who fear Him,

and His righteousness to children's children,

to such as keep His covenant,

and to those who remember

His commandments to do them.

PSALM 103:17–18, NKJV

THE SECRET TO A SUCCESSFUL, THRIVING FAMILY

A great marriage provides optimal conditions for a child to do well. And a child's success often contributes to the health of a marriage. My many years of clinical work have confirmed to me that the best way to build great families is to build great marriages. I am aware of how vitally children can contribute to a marriage, but an unhealthy marriage seldom gets healthy on the basis of the success of the children. And children are seldom emotionally healthy or happy when their parents are not well loved by each other.

The secret of a well-connected family system is almost always a function of a carefully nurtured love relationship between the two parents. Keeping this love relationship in the best emotional shape is the fundamental challenge for every man and woman who ventures into the family-building business.

And these words, which I am commanding you today, shall be on your heart; and you shall teach them diligently to your sons and shall talk of them when you sit in your house and when you walk by the way and when you lie down and when you rise up.

DEUTERONOMY 6:6–7, NASB

*P*arents who are successful tell me that no other principle is as important as realizing that, as a parent, you are a "trustee." You do not own your children. You have them for only a short while, and then they will leave you.

This means, of course, that you should not try to make them into a carbon copy of yourself. It is all right to give them your name if you choose, but it is not all right to expect that they will be just like you. They may become remarkably different from you. They have a separate identity, they are created with a different biochemical system from any person on earth, they have unique personalities, and they will ultimately determine their own destiny. They are separate beings!

So realize that you are a trustee only—not an owner.

I have also dedicated him to the Lord;

as long as he lives he is dedicated to the Lord.

1 Samuel 1:28, NASB

PINPOINTING YOUR CHILD'S TALENTS

A fundamental part of your parenting task is to help your child discover his or her talents, strengths, interests, gifts, and natural abilities. This discovery often requires listening on the part of parents. Great parents listen to gain information about their child's essential likes and dislikes, interests, needs, hurts, and hopes. This process also takes keen observation as you watch and determine where your child's natural talents lie.

Once identified, these talents must be nurtured and cultivated. You must give your child the opportunity to grow and expand. It is your job to help your child reach his or her full potential.

When parents handle this task conscientiously, their child's eventual identity will once more reflect the awesome creativity of the Creator. And the relationship that will develop between these parents and this little child will be rich and satisfying. When the task of parenting is done right, there is nothing like it in the world. One of its finest by-products is that it makes two parents grow together as they never have before.

A new commandment I give to you,

that you love one another,

even as I have loved you,

that you also love one another.

JOHN 13:34, NASB

LOVING YOUR CHILD—UNCONDITIONALLY

*A*bsolutely nothing is more important to psychological development than a child's basic sense that his or her worth is never in jeopardy, that he is loved simply because of who he is—not on the basis of any conditional factors. Love isn't given and taken away because of behavior, performance, intellect, appearance, academic achievement, or any other component. Love is just given—no questions asked, nothing demanded in return. It is this experience that will allow him to develop to the full extent of his capacity.

But parents are able to love their child unconditionally only to the degree to which they have experienced unconditional love themselves. I have found that I can love this way only when I keep myself strong in my own Christian faith. My parents instilled within me a deep belief that I have been created by a God who loves me to my depths, who could love me no more deeply if I were perfect and no less strongly if I were totally imperfect.

When I stay in touch with this dynamic, my ability to love unconditionally the people around me becomes greater.

For the Lord gives wisdom;

from His mouth come knowledge and understanding.

He stores up sound wisdom for the upright;

He is a shield to those who walk in integrity.

PROVERBS 2:6-7, NASB

SETTING—AND MAINTAINING—LIMITS

*I*t is essential that parents place limits on their children's behavior. These limits give their children a sense of security, and they protect both the parents and others from out-of-control children.

The determination of these limits is clearly of great importance. If they are set too narrowly or unrealistically, the child will be filled with frustration and resentment. But limits can also be set too broadly, resulting in excessive permissiveness that is not at all good for child, parent, or others.

I recommend that parents spend generous amounts of time in the determination of limits for their children, seek the best advice they can, work hard to agree on what these limits should be, and then be highly consistent in maintaining these limits.

For we are God's workmanship,

created in Christ Jesus

to do good works,

which God prepared

in advance for us to do.

EPHESIANS 2:10, NIV

DREAMING WITH YOUR CHILD

*P*arents are in a prime position to help their children develop
a dream for their lives. Just as parents need a great dream
for their marriage, so do children need a life dream. This dream
can be modified all along the way, but any dream will stimulate
their brains and mobilize their action centers.

Moreover, there is nothing two parents can do for their marriage
that will inspire them more than helping their children develop
goals—goals that will set them free to stretch and grow as they actu-
alize their potential. Show me a young person with a wonderful
dream, and I will show you some active and satisfied parents in the
background.

Train up a child in the way he should go:

and when he is old, he will not depart from it.

PROVERBS 22:6, KJV

DEVELOPING YOUR CHILD'S CHARACTER AND VALUES

I know of nothing that is quite so gratifying for parents as recognizing that their child has developed attributes of character that will strengthen him for a lifetime. Likewise, when a child identifies values in which he passionately believes and for which he is willing to give his all, both parents and child can be deeply thankful and proud.

Of course, one of the strongest evidences of sterling character is the way the child treats others in the family, including younger siblings and older relatives. Sensitivity in these areas is a sign of deep security, thoughtful reflection, and good judgment.

As for me and my house,

we will serve the Lord.

JOSHUA 24:15, KJV

THE FABRIC OF FAMILY

When there is love between a husband and wife, and where there is strong respect for the children born out of that love, the result is sure to be a family that can relate to one another in deeply meaningful ways. When this kind of connectedness happens within a secure atmosphere, the many shades of love that result almost always make for an overwhelmingly beautiful human fabric. We call this fabric a family.

When there is a dad who loves a mom with a durable, undying love, and when a mom loves a dad with a soft, pure, never-ending affection, the children are sure to benefit greatly.

A triumphant marriage is the context in which any baby would like to find himself or herself. These children will grow up to be emotionally, physically, mentally, spiritually, and socially strong—and they will make any marriage even more triumphant.

PART FIVE

FELLOW TRAVELERS
on a Spiritual Journey

W hen two lovers are both spiritually sensitive, I suspect their marriage is destined to be triumphant. What an incredible difference it makes to both of them to know that they are fellow travelers on a spiritual journey.

When a couple becomes spiritually healthy, they automatically move toward marital harmony and oneness. There is something miraculously bonding for two lovers when they experience significant overlap in the spiritual realm.

As a clinician who has worked with couples for three decades, I know that you can't talk about a triumphant marriage without including the spiritual dimension. And the one hundred couples I surveyed confirmed this. They said that one of the key secrets for a great marriage is the ability of a couple to "plumb their spiritual depths."

If one prevail against him,

two shall withstand him;

and a threefold cord is not quickly broken.

ECCLESIASTES 4:12, KJV

When two people cling to each other in a crisis and pour out their feelings to a God they both trust and love, there is a merging and blending that weaves them together at their deepest levels. As a matter of fact, I'm convinced that spirituality is especially beneficial for a couple when it involves the deeper ranges of their thinking and feeling—the parts of their life-processing that are far below the superficial levels on which they sometimes operate.

These deeper levels that get drawn into the spiritual search are especially crucial because they often involve life situations in which we feel unusually desperate, deeply inadequate, intensely in need of help from someone with power and understanding well beyond our own.

That's why a married couple profits so much when they can spiritually process life together—when they can speak together to God and are forced to put into words inexpressible hopes and feelings. In that moment, they touch each other at their depths and become welded together far more significantly.

So God created man in his own image,

in the image of God created he him;

male and female created he them.

Genesis 1:27, KJV

A PASSIONATE QUEST

*I*nterestingly, sexuality and spirituality, I believe, overlap to a surprising degree. They both involve intimate parts of our beings. We must be healthy and secure in these parts of ourselves if we are to have a triumphant marriage. Both sexuality and spirituality participate in that level of our inner selves where our deepest feelings exist.

Why is it so important for a marriage that people be in harmony when it comes to extremely strong feelings? That's where life really matters! That's where we desperately want to share life with the person we love and respect the most. It is intimacy taken to the deepest level, intimacy that is richer and purer than any other form of intimacy we know.

This is the reason any couple who develops their capacity to share their spiritual quests is destined to have a triumphant marriage. The two lovers overcome the greatest of all marital enemies—emotional distance. They become joined and interwoven right where they are most wonderfully made.

Before I formed you in the womb I knew you,

and before you were born I consecrated you.

JEREMIAH 1:5, NASB

A VIEW THROUGH GOD'S EYES

I believe the primary motivation for every person on earth is a universal and powerful desire to feel good about himself or herself. From a very early stage in our development, we adopt strategies for bringing this about. We may crave independence or ownership, feel competitive, or be needy. But these strategies don't work well within a marriage.

However, the strategy for acquiring a self-conception that does work is as old as the Bible. It has to do with getting yourself into a right relationship with God. That requires that we let him be God and that we get about the task of discovering and being the persons we really are. This strategy stresses that we have been created with great worth and that we don't have to produce more value for ourselves. It is our calling to try to fulfill our enormous potential. When we do this, we discover the excitement and satisfaction that come from exploring our uniqueness and living it out.

You are a chosen people, a royal priesthood,

a holy nation, a people belonging to God,

that you may declare the praises of him

who called you out of darkness

into his wonderful light.

1 Peter 2:9, NIV

ENLARGING YOUR ENVIRONMENT

*H*ow do you enlarge the environment in which your marriage exists? How do you keep your relationship from becoming boring?

How about starting with the spiritual? Move out of your narrowly focused world, and aim your sights toward the larger world—and the world beyond the larger world. For instance, get involved with an active, enthusiastic church. How might that contribute to the scope of your lives and the energy of your daily existence?

First, you will be drawn into a lively dialogue about the most crucial issues involved in living. You'll be challenged to think about your role on earth and who is in charge of this world and have the opportunity to get to know this sovereign being better. You'll be singing and praying and laughing and thinking and feeling more deeply than before. You will be caring more passionately. You will come alive individually—and in your marriage!

Then life no longer can be humdrum.

For where two or three

are gathered together in My name,

I am there in the midst of them.

<small>MATTHEW 18:20, NKJV</small>

EXPERIENCING GOD—TOGETHER

When I find couples who can be spiritual together—who worship, study, sing, pray, cry, laugh, and talk together—I know they have a great chance of making something special between them.

When conversations at dinner are filled with current events, concern for the world, and discussion about Bible passages, there is no end of excitement that can be generated.

Show me a family that talks around the dinner table about what they're learning about God and the importance of caring about other people in the world, and I'll show you a family that is alive and healthy.

Spirituality is crucial for any couple and any couple's family. As they experience God together, they will have minds and hearts that are eager for tomorrow morning to come.

Whatever is true, whatever is noble,

whatever is right, whatever is pure,

whatever is lovely, whatever is admirable—

if anything is excellent or praiseworthy—

think about such things.

PHILIPPIANS 4:8, NIV

SEARCHING FOR THE PERFECT BALANCE

*M*any struggles can arise when a couple dedicates themselves to pursuing spiritual meaning. One of the most constant has to do with the struggle between thinking and feeling. Couples who spend too much time thinking together often lack emotional vitality in their marriage. On the other hand, people who are too deeply into feeling and experiencing suffer from an absence of cognitive structure for their lives—a structure that provides organization and tends to hold life together when things get temporarily out of control.

So how do you develop this kind of balance in a marriage? First, you recognize it as a goal. Then you think and feel your way to the goal. You pursue writings, teachings, art, music, movies, and plays that help you develop one part or another of this goal. And you watch to make sure you don't drift too far in one of these directions. In your searching, seek for a healthy balance between thinking and feeling.

For God so loved the world

that He gave His only begotten Son,

that whoever believes in Him

should not perish

but have everlasting life.

John 3:16, NKJV

MOVING TOWARD A RIGHT RELATIONSHIP

*T*he New Testament apostles Paul and John suggest that we can determine whether a person is "in a right relationship with God" or "is filled with the Holy Spirit."

Paul lists the "fruit of the Spirit": love, joy, peace, patience, kindness, goodness, faithfulness, gentleness, and self-control. If a person demonstrates these qualities, would you say that he is emotionally healthy? Certainly. And if these qualities were missing or were seldom demonstrated, you would probably question that person's emotional health.

John takes a very similar approach. He says that you become triumphant in your personal struggles when "Christ lives in you." In fact, John says: "Anyone who claims to be in the light but hates his brother is still in the darkness" (1 John 2:9, NIV). For John, emotional and spiritual health are, I believe, virtually synonymous, and you can tell when "health" has happened—you gain a deep sense of concern and love for others.

You will seek Me and find Me,

when you search for Me with all your heart.

JEREMIAH 29:13, NASB

When a man and woman turn their attention to spiritual wholeness, they will be moving inevitably toward emotional health as well. You can't have one without the other.

But there is one caveat. It takes a while for this inner change to occur. A person can be filled with the Holy Spirit and thus be spiritually healthy, while emotional health still needs to grow. The old habituated defense patterns may take some time to dissolve.

However, no person can get into a right relationship with themselves and others until they have gotten into a right relationship with God.

No marriage can be truly triumphant until both parties are individually "right" with themselves. If this latter state requires a "right relationship with God," it seems obvious that a great marriage requires two people who have reached a deep level of spiritual health.

Do not lay up for yourselves treasures on earth,

where moth and rust destroy

and where thieves break in and steal;

but lay up for yourselves treasures in heaven. . . .

For where your treasure is,

there your heart will be also.

MATTHEW 6:19–21, NKJV

A SPIRITUAL PERSPECTIVE

*T*he whole discussion about spirituality boils down to this: The world we live in every day, what we call the material world, largely involves the external—that which is outside our skin. If we try to build a great marriage that focuses exclusively on the material world, the foundation will be shallow.

But spirituality involves what is inside. It is built around a quest for deeper meaning, for a clearer sense about profound and eternal matters. Marriages that involve two people who share their experiences, thoughts, concerns, and involvement in these areas of life tend to hold together and become richer over time. These marriages usually are extremely close and ultimately healthy.

It is, then, this moving away from the material world and into the spiritual realm that takes a marriage from the superficial to the profound, from the immediate to the eternal, from two distinct individuals to two who merge into "one flesh." In the process, their relationship becomes stronger, larger, more colorful, and more satisfying.

Now to Him who is able to do exceeding abundantly

beyond all that we ask or think, according to the power

that works within us, to Him be the glory.

EPHESIANS 3:20-21, NASB

TRANSFORMING YOUR MARRIAGE

*M*arriages are incredibly complex! You can't revolutionize them overnight, but you can move them from ordinary to magnificent over time and through hard work. Nothing as valuable as a great marriage is going to be delivered to you on a silver platter. You get the privilege of creating it yourselves.

If you can say in your heart, *I am ready for my marriage to start moving toward greatness, and I'll do what it takes to make it happen,* you are on the brink of an exciting adventure. All you need is willingness, determination, commitment—and the ability to tell the truth in love.

If you make sure that you are loyal and true to your spouse in everything you do, your marriage will be grounded in granite. It will be held together by steel. It will last forever. And, best of all, it will allow you to know on this earth that level of love that is woven into God himself—and it will last throughout the ages!